Boo-hoo, Baby!

First published in 2009
by Wayland

This paperback edition published in 2010 by Wayland

Wayland
338 Euston Road
London NW1 3BH

Wayland Australia
Level 17/207 Kent Street
Sydney, NSW 2000

Series Editor: Louise John
Editor: Katie Powell
Cover design: Paul Cherrill
Design: D.R.ink
Consultant: Shirley Bickler

A CIP catalogue record for this book is available from the British Library.

ISBN 9780750259125 (hbk)
ISBN 9780750259309 (pbk)

Printed in China

Wayland is a division of Hachette Children's Books,
an Hachette UK Company

www.hachette.co.uk

Boo-hoo, Baby!

Written by Claire Llewellyn
Illustrated by Polona Lovšin

WAYLAND

I looked at the dog.
Baby looked at
the dog too.

I looked at the duck.
Baby looked at
the duck too.

I looked at the cow.
Baby looked at
the cow too.

I looked at the sheep.
Baby looked at
the sheep too.

I looked at the pig.
Baby looked at
the pig too.

13

I looked at the cat.
Baby looked at
the cat too.

I looked at the hen.
Baby looked at
the hen too.

I looked at the horse.
Baby looked at
the horse too.

I looked at the ice creams.
Baby looked at the
ice creams too.

Baby said, "Ooooh!"

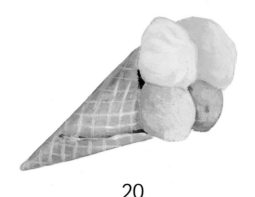

Guiding a First Read
Boo-hoo, Baby!

It is important to talk through the book with the child before they attempt to read it alone. This will build confidence and enable the child to tackle the first read without feeling overwhelmed. Look at the pictures together, read the book title, and pick out words of interest and the high frequency words for discussion.

The high frequency words in this title are:
at   I   looked   the

1. Talking through the book

The boy looked at all the animals at the farm. But Baby just kept crying, "Boo-hoo!"

Let's read the title: Boo-hoo, Baby!
Turn to page 4. The boy said, "I looked at the dog. Baby looked at the dog too."
Now look at the picture. "Woof! Woof!" said the dog. "Boo-hoo!" said the baby.

Now turn to page 6. What do you think the boy says on this page?

Continue to read the book, with the child looking at the illustrations, for example on page 20:

Why do you think Baby stopped crying? Yes, Baby saw the ice creams. Baby said, "Ooooh!"

2. A first reading of the book

Ask the child to read the book independently and point carefully underneath each word (tracking), while thinking about the story.

Work with the child, prompting them and praising their careful tracking, attempts to correct themselves and their knowledge of letters and sounds, for example:

> **I like the way you checked the pictures first and then pointed carefully as you read.**
> **It could be 'chicken' but that word starts with 'h'.**
> **What else could it be? Sound out the letters.**

3. Follow-up activities

· Select a high frequency word, as listed on p22, and ask the child to find it throughout the book. Discuss the shape of the letters and the letter sounds.

· To memorise the word, ask the child to write it in the air, then write it repeatedly on a whiteboard or on paper, leaving a space between each attempt.

· Alternate writing the new word starting with a capital letter, and then with a lower-case letter.

4. Encourage

· Rereading of the book many times.

· Drawing a picture based on the story.

· Writing a sentence using the practised word.

START READING is a series of highly enjoyable books for beginner readers. **The books have been carefully graded to match the Book Bands widely used in schools.** This enables readers to be sure they choose books that match their own reading ability.

Look out for the Band colour on the book in our Start Reading logo.

The Bands are:

Pink Band 1A and 1B

Red Band 2

Yellow Band 3

Blue Band 4

Green Band 5

Orange Band 6

Turquoise Band 7

Purple Band 8

Gold Band 9

START READING books can be read independently or shared with an adult. They promote the enjoyment of reading through satisfying stories supported by fun illustrations.

Claire Llewellyn has written many books for children. Some of them are about real things like animals and the Moon, others are storybooks. Claire has two children, but they are getting too big for stories like this one. She hopes you will enjoy reading her stories instead.

Polona Lovšin was born in Ljubljana, Slovenia in 1973. She graduated from the Academy of Fine Arts in Ljubljana. Polona loves to draw people, especially children and finds that each new book brings many challenges but lots of fun, too!